FUCHSIA IN CAMBODIA

ROY JACOBSTEIN

FUCHSIA IN CAMBODIA

POEMS

TriQuarterly Books
Northwestern University Press
Evanston, Illinois

TriQuarterly Books
Northwestern University Press
www.nupress.northwestern.edu

Printed in the United States of America

10   9   8   7   6   5   4   3   2   1

Library of Congress Cataloging-in-Publication Data

Jacobstein, Roy.
    Fuchsia in Cambodia / Roy Jacobstein.
      p. cm.
    ISBN-13: 978-0-8101-5202-1 (cloth : alk. paper)
    ISBN-10: 0-8101-5202-9 (cloth : alk. paper)
    ISBN-13: 978-0-8101-5201-4 (pbk. : alk. paper)
    ISBN-10: 0-8101-5201-0 (pbk. : alk. paper)
  I. Title.
  PS3610.A3568F83 2008
  811'.6—dc22

2007044166

♾ The paper used in this publication meets the minimum requirements of the American
National Standard for Information Sciences—Permanence of Paper for Printed Library
Materials, ANSI Z39.48-1992.

For Sophie-Anne and David,
and for Linda, closest reader

Beginning my studies the first step pleas'd me so much,
The mere fact consciousness, these forms, the power of motion,
The least insect or animal, the senses, eyesight, love . . .

—Walt Whitman

CONTENTS

THREE

FOUR

ACKNOWLEDGMENTS

Grateful acknowledgment is made to the editors of the following publications where these poems, some of which have been revised, first appeared:

Arts & Letters: "Nick of Time"

88: "The Taste of Guava"

Gettysburg Review: "Conundrum"; "How to Thrive in the Office Cube"; "If They Don't Have Ritalin in Heaven,"; "Working Out"

Green Mountains Review: "The Ride"

Hayden's Ferry Review: "Puberty"

Iowa Review: "Heaven"; "Ode to Stegosaurus"

JAMA: "The Taj"

Michigan Quarterly Review: "Dilemma"

Mid-American Review: "A.R.T."

Mississippi Review: "Woman Needs Man" (as "Note to You from Kathmandu")

Missouri Review: "License"; "Round Trip"; "Still"

Prairie Schooner: "Bad Buddhist"; "Cold Chop"; "Passing Customs"; "Phlox"; "Spinning Bottle"

Quarterly West: "Air and All"

Rattle: "Sustenance"

Shenandoah: "Adams-Morgan Aubade"

TriQuarterly: "Ceremony"; "First Egg"; "Papaya"; "The Persistence of Memory"; "Referral"; "The Unknown Albeit, or While Reading a Friend's Prizewinning Book on Love's Vicissitudes He Writes About Words"

"If They Don't Have Ritalin in Heaven," received special mention in the 2007 Pushcart Prize anthology.

"How to Thrive in the Office Cube" was featured in the business section of the *Raleigh News and Observer* in 2007.

"Heaven" and "Ode to Stegosaurus" were runners-up for the 2005 *Iowa Review* Poetry Award.

"Air and All"; "How to Thrive in the Office Cube"; "If They Don't Have Ritalin in Heaven,"; "Nick of Time"; "The Persistence of Memory"; "Puberty"; "The Taste of Guava"; and "Working Out" appeared in *Tourniquet* (Hollyridge Press Chapbook Series, 2005).

"Puberty" was runner-up for the 2003 *Indiana Review* Poetry Prize.

Special thanks to my friends in poetry: Rick Bursky, Alex Grant, George Higgins, Edward Hirsch, Jane Hirshfield, Gary Lilley, Thomas Lux, Margaret Rabb, Greg Rappleye, Robert Thomas, Eleanor Wilner, and Ian Wilson; and to Linda Gregerson, Platonic ideal of teacher and mentor become friend.

FUCHSIA IN CAMBODIA

ONE

The Persistence of Memory

Having once heard the streetcar
we can still hear its clang here
on this strand where languor

is counterpoint in its stillness
to the silver waves that break
against, and fall from, the rocks,

until the silence again descends
into the finitude it takes for,
once more, the waves to break,

recalling the streetcar, its torque,
its screech and roar, the electric air,
which would fill one with wonder

at the varied sound of the world,
that furious clang, that is there,
then gone, into silence, then back.

Ode to Stegosaurus

That magnificent cascade of convenient paired plates—
not only were they his central heating and cooling, Jurassic
to mid-Cretaceous, but countless 20th century kids passed
their lengthy laughing hour in museums great or small
or in parks verdant or bare, sequestered snugly there.
How many of the adults they've become must still possess
their bronze or plastic replica, once boon companion
that shared bed and board and primal fear (of Allosaurus,
T. rex—those implacable, giant-thighed flesh-devourers,
stalactite- and stalagmite-teeth ready to tear the instant
Mom turned out the lights).
                                        O Roof Lizard, stalwart
walnut-brained ten-ton friend, rotund muncher of fronds
and leaves, state fossil of Colorado, what hath they wrought,
these paleontologists bent on revision? They've made you
more sleek, as if you'd been subjected to serial diet fads
and they all took. They've shrunk your plates, wiped out
your stolid symmetry fore and aft by raising your hind legs,
jacking up your underbelly from the soft green ground.
We've lost the promise of your familiar body: *Come, ride me
into darkness, I will carry you and protect you with my many-spiked tail
and lick your wounds clean with my grass-loving tongue.*

Puberty

I call my film *Still Life*
with Platypus and Wind Chimes
because the *us* in *platypus*
and the idea of a marsupial's
pouch are both symbolic.
At least that's how I pitched it
to the studio. But I lied—the film
has no platypus, no symbols, no wind
chimes. Just a twelve-year-old kid
in a greasy spoon somewhere
out West, patties of meat being
spatulaed off the spitting grill,
cigarette haze encasing the diners,
and he sees the frantic trapped
moth banging against the screen,
and we see the moth in extreme
close-up, trying to get out, back
into the sweet evening air,
so the kid bolts from the red
leather booth, his family
eating chicken-fried steaks,
and makes for the screen door,
pushes it open, gently
flicks the moth back out
into Wyoming or Colorado,
sees it ascend, sees the black
beak of a bird zap it away.
Then we cut from his stunned
face to the busty waitress:
the banana split is coming.

Cold Chop

Muzak overhead. He resists it long
as he can, then discerns *Beyond
the Sea,* oldie that unicycled his brain
nonstop during its season of yearning
for the unknowable and blithe object
of his geek-teen crush. He wanted *her*
by his side not his father and brother,
the three of them at water's edge,
skipping stones into the cold chop
of Green Bay. Those futile throes
shadow him still, casting their pall
over every wave, lesson she taught
in time and distance: you can ford
umpteen zones, fly beyond any sea,
but longing's always the hammer-
head shark, and you, you're nothing
but the pilotfish, ingesting the waste.

Nick of Time

Wasn't it only yesterday father & son bent low
    over two squares of sidewalk to play hand tennis,
        volley the yellow fuzzy ball off their palms, curve

it away from each other toward the unmown lawn?
    All those trips to the roundhouse, to sight the boxcars
        clacketing west toward the sun. Dusk in Boulder meant

Addis Ababa eyeing the moon, high in a starlit sky.
    The family outing to the Anasazi ruins at Mesa Verde
        was yet to come, now is past. My ride to the airport,

once to come, is passing fast. This time the driver's
    not an exiled Iranian economist, not a Nigerian chieftain's
        son from some wrong tribe, he's Abebe, named to honor

Abebe Bikele, Africa's first Olympic champion, who
    ran Rome's stone streets 26.2 miles, that precise distance
        athletes ran 25 centuries ago at Marathon to Pindar's praise,

but Abebe ran barefoot, as our Pleistocene ancestors
    must have run (toward their prey, or prey themselves),
        & four years later, now shod, in innocent Tokyo, 1964,

again he inclined his neck forward, black swan
    accepting the victor's gold (less than three years
        until the car crash will paralyze him, waist-down).

He was so tall & handsome, his namesake says,
    & now the women of my country win too, leading
        me to Cleopatra, what she looked like, & the asp,

which breast it bit, how long it lingered there,
    how long the poison took, & those wind-borne
        dhows, do they still ply the eternal Nile (pyramids

& bulrushes & crocodiles, riven green ribbon
    slicing the desert, crotch to crown), & that busload
        of German tourists, were they slaughtered before

or after they saw the Temple of Karnak & why
    is the Lower Nile above the Upper, at least on maps
        of our one known home—& when the plane lands

in a new time zone, & a refugee or a refugee's son
    from Algeria or Cambodia drives me past the Ford plant
        where I worked in '76 (summer welder among the lifers)

onward to William Beaumont Hospital, Royal Oak,
    Michigan, will my father's bony hand still be clutching
        his IV pole, the piss-yellow chemo ripping into his veins,

will any of his once-black hair remain, will he still
    recognize me, & if I keep at it forty-three more years
        can I make a work of art, even beauty, from this jumble

we call *the world*—yellow balls & summer lawns, temples
    & tourists, exiles, IV poles, crocodiles—& may it stay
        the confusion & the madness, Lord, if not the clock.

Spinning Bottle

—Eugene Zuckman, friend at 12

Where have you wandered
in this widening world?
There must be a megalopolis
of memories imprinted upon
those neurons of your limbic lobe
where event and smell entwine
like newlyweds. Inhale once,
you're back: the dark-veneered
floors, the musty corridors
suffused with the immigrant
waft of cooked cabbage,
the light dim throughout
your mother's flat, as if cutting
wattage could bring your father back.
Who knocked first, gap-toothed Ruth,
still a half-head taller than us?
Did we eat anything, or just drop
to the floor? It's all gone opaque
save that empty Coke bottle
sighting its slow sure way
toward me: eyes shut,
lips protruding, waiting,
waiting. Have you found yourself
looking for her, Eugene,
out on the dance floor?
Do you protrude your lips too,
hoping the perfect lips
of Phyllis Glist touch yours
again, hoping this time
you'll know what to do?

Round Trip

1. Outbound

Going back
to Detroit, a place
I've been running from
since I learned to run.
Ran from the black boys.
Ran from the white boys.
Ran to the chain-link end
of the gravel playground.
Ran from the palsied girl
I wanted to run to (her
constantly cycling head,
her locked-in smile).
Back to the city of rust,
city of bone. Going
to the last brother
of my father, to his 19 pills
and still the organs fail.
City of carburetor, camshaft,
hubcap, lug nut: Detroit,
Detroit, where the weak
are chewed and eaten,
Detroit, I'm running
straight for your mouth.

2. Descent

Knifing through 22,000 feet,
I can't be the only one
who gets the urge,
seated in the emergency EXIT row,
to leap up REMOVE COVER
                    AND
            PULL HANDLE
—can I? Just put aside
the Rold Gold fat-free pretzels
and step out, tetherless,
into the icy patina of blue,
temperature -48° Celsius,
the drone of the engine
taunting us, egging us on—*Come,*
feel what it's like: that moment
before the earth tightens its grip
on your final descent, your seats
upright, seat belts locked into place,
luggage securely stowed
in the overhead compartment,
before you taxi the runway, terra
firma again, some tan Dodge
or gray Ford waiting for you
in the auto rental lot.

3. Return

From beyond the doorway
    of the delicatessen the redolence
        of the Roumanian pastrami

bathing our olfactory bulbs
    and the certainty of half-dill pickles
        luxuriating in their barrel

of brine impel us onward. Ah,
    kugel, knishes, the matzo-ball soup . . .
        if ethnicity in America's

been reduced to food, thank God
    the chopped liver's still saturated
        with chicken fat, that gold

the world dismisses as *schmaltz*—
    this thought, numinous, fleeting, occurs
        in a trice, conflated: the door

has opened wide: a beaming
    mother, sated on latkes, her infant
        joey-ed upon her chest,

steps out, blinking
    into the warmth of the latest
        late spring sun,

while the birthday boy,
    Uncle Ray, former tank commander
        under Patton, ninety-one

today, leads us in, gripping
    the gleaming metal bar of his walker
        and inhaling the pastrami

with each advance he makes.

TWO

Adams-Morgan Aubade

Birdsong beyond the bedroom
    window, and the greening rush
        of the leaves, and everywhere

we go, we drive, so you tell all
    your Soho pals you've moved
        to the suburbs and well into fall

you cull your aromatic Thai basil
    from our communal plot's parsley
        and chive, to spice your fiery wok.

You know no neighborhood in D.C.
    comes closer to New York, its islands
        of immigrants, its tongues and cuisines.

(Dominicans hawking mangoes, rosaries,
    merengue tapes; Rastas in tricolored berets
        syncopating *One Love;* the ceviche, falafel,

döner kebap.) But you're homesick,
    and where this Rust Belt refugee fits,
        I don't ask, I just press the humid air

between us until we're nothing
    but the basil, the wok, and the flame.

Working Out

There will always be that fear.
Your lover pumps iron, jogs
with you in the park.
Still, the needles hiss when you pass,
they know your route, how you slow
before the reservoir, then burst
onto the gravel path. Who are you kidding,
when each stride brings you no closer to the finish.
No wonder you can't relax,
afraid to breathe, afraid to see
your shadow lengthen on the pavement
like a flash flood filling an empty riverbed.

The Ride

Will this be another ride of the future past,
the bluebottle fly buzzing up the window
of this airport bus to Delhi, those placid
skeletal cows wedged into the inner circle
of the roundabout, & this elegant woman

sitting beside me in her nimbus of jasmine-
scent & royal purple sari possess the same
numinousness years hence (the mysterious
lasting conflation) as does that other ride
taken twenty-odd years ago in Taormina,

when I first saw the coarse underarm hairs
curling out from the woman's black blouse
as we all held fast to the overhead straps
in summer's haze while the bus shimmied
& we swayed & beyond the open windows

drying shirts & sheets flapped & fluttered
on balconies & little orange & yellow cars
buzzed by & suddenly I realized women
grew hair *there* too, & my stop was far off,
beyond the city walls, up into the hills?

Woman Needs Man

In a far district, where every week
Sherpas routinely conquered Everest,
unreconstructed Maoists assault

another police barracks, while here,
despite the coils, the smoke, the rank
Jungle Cream, another tiny anopheline

has pierced the porous perimeter
of my defenses. So in this milieu
of bullock cart and chakra, prayer

wheel and dust, opaque white eyes,
I will await the onset of the exquisite
ague, meditate until lysis commences

upon the fading graffito paint-sprayed
on the flank of the Yak and Yeti Hotel:
Woman needs man like hawk needs rickshaw.

How to Thrive in the Office Cube

Make peace
    with the space
        you're dealt, be

a beacon
    of equanimity
        and competence,

set out
    the photographs
        of Dad, the dog,

the day
    you sailed
        the blue bay.

With respect
    to your voice, don't
        lower it

more than two octaves,
    though it will
        behoove you

to call
    your new lover
        from a private phone.

And instead,
    should he
        call you, say

"*Mon ange,*
    your eyes are
        the glowing coals

in the blast furnace
    that is my heart,"
        you must respond

coolly
    with "Yes,
        Steve, the report

is coming along fine
    and will be available
        for your perusal

by COB today."
    Such dispassion
        has useful spill-

over: the dry cleaner
    will give you the discount
        even though you forgot

the coupon.
    The mechanic notorious
        for gouging

his customers
    will fear you
        know something

and not overcharge.
    Your landlord will promptly
        repair the heat pump.

And your lover,
    who may
        or may not be

Steve, will take
    your demeanor for
        the deep still ardor

he has been meant
    to unlock all his life,
        beginning with dinner

at the little
    Turkish place
        where he will order

meze and raki
    and ask you
        "Are you always

this cool?"

Sustenance

They seem a little molecule of calm
in a charged field of gray clucking,
this raggedy couple holding hands

while tossing handfuls of pretzel bits
like ticker tape into converging coveys
on Broadway & 43rd. Doesn't she know

they have the worst glycemic index
of any snack food, even pork rinds?
And he's as oblivious to the people

breezing by on foot and bike and skate
and the nuclear news looming in neon
overhead as are the pigeons to the havoc

those morsels wreak on waistlines.
But they're content in their self-
absorbed way, and when I pivot

my head I cannot see anybody else
offering the promise of sustenance,
so I waddle over to them, start pecking.

License

Keeping my mind on love today
    as I drive down Connecticut to G,
        past the warrens of condominiums,

past the anonymous blocks
    of eight-story office buildings where
        the hundred thousand lawyers toil

(if that trusty Anglo-Saxon verb
    can be used for *depose* and *litigate*),
        so I stop to marvel at the sun back-

lighting the gaggle of Canada geese
    wending alphabetically across the sky—
        great grey honkers who mate for life—

now a *w,* now a *v,* who's the leader
    I wonder, and how do they know
        which inlet of Hudson Bay to call

home, which long path is free
    of the hunters' gauged steel,
        and how many ganders are part

of that gaggle, and how many
    gaggles make a googol—always
        this battle inside my yipping beagle

of a brain between how many
    and how lovely, between the stone
        and the shimmer, between the cloud-

refracted beams of golden dust
    and everything we'd ever need
        to know about the sun: lone star,

accident, 93 million miles out—
    and stars burn out, all of them,
        thousands more extinguished

each night: *poof,* no longer there,
    wherever *there* is, or was, though
        their light shines on, iridescent

beaded thread of the infinite
    celestial quilt, a googol of stars,
        each one nothing but gaseous mass

and filigreed edge, burning
    a hundred thousand star-years
        into the essentially empty universe,

in one nook of a random speck
    of which I'm passing, anon, through
        the metal detector in the lobby, past

the uniformed guard, up the center
    elevator, *eighth floor, second right,* where
        your gap-toothed grin and our license

to wed merge in delight.

The Taj

They tell you it's a Wonder, a memorial
to love (Shah Jahan for Mumtaz, his wife,
and perhaps, by extension, of all men
for their wives, and vice versa, why not,
even for the very concept of Love,
and not only the Earthly),
that words can never do it justice
nor the glossy photos in the coffee table books;
plus there's the poignant fact
Jahan was imprisoned across the river
by his son, Aurangzeb, just before
the dome was finally joined, and thus condemned
to view the finished edifice he'd never entered
every day those last few years of his long life.
So you show up at 6 A.M., part
the burgeoning horde of vendors,
already your sweat-soaked shirt's
glommed to your back, and lo!: shimmering
at a distance, immaculate
white marble and twinned waterborne white reflection
filling the archway with that roseate glow,
taking everyone's breath and yours
as it was meant to do. But they don't tell you
Mumtaz had fourteen children and died in childbirth
at thirty-eight, and Jahan had many other wives
who comforted him
and bore him many children
while he held dominion two more decades
before Aurangzeb began to reign.

A.R.T.*

Medicated, tense, unmoving, silent,

you lie supine, legs splayed, no doubt

willing the sad similitude away—

but how penis-like that catheter seems

on the fluoroscope screen as the Doctor

in his crisp and immaculate white coat

advances it into your uterus, stealing

your breath. Like those sleek *smart bombs*

shown over and over in the televised wars,

that snuff the embedded foe and leave

the structure wholly hollowed of animal life

yet otherwise complete, intact, good to go.

---

*Assisted Reproductive Technology

THREE

Referral

Digitized, the photo arrives
through cyberspace—and there
she is: your daughter,
in bountiful cap of natal hair.
Black eyes fixed on the unseen
photographer's flash, tiny garnet
lips poised to arc into smile,
she exudes the utter confidence
of the newly born, and your milkless
breasts swell and you wonder
do they have fuchsia
in Cambodia, and frangipani,
and if so, what are they called,
with what syllables pronounced,
how soon will you learn them,
and how well?

The Golden Door

—Newark, 10/22/01

In two years you'll be calling
what took us to the rear commode
an *SUV poop,* the age-old processes
of evacuation and cognition proceeding
blithely apace. The few other passengers
on our jumbo jet returned from Asia
deplaned long ago to degrees of fear
this flawless fall Monday cannot ease.
The Garden State when we departed
last month, now it's *Anthrax Capital
of America.* We're the only ones clearing
customs in this airport renamed *Liberty.*
Spores pock the re-entry terminal's
sterile walls. New daughter, the gift
of citizenship's being bestowed. Welcome
to your new land. We would follow
your smile but the door is locked.
I throw you into the air. It cracks open,
permitting a shaft of light
to illuminate the counter, the dust.

Ceremony

At the end of the blessing
ceremony held for you
at the neighborhood *wat*
on the rutted dirt road
near the Silver Palace,
after the monk had chanted
his sacred Pali texts
in a steady bass monotone
(for what seemed three hours
to my creaking knees)
and sprinkled your head
with what I imagined
to be lotus-water,
he pulled his cell phone
from beneath his saffron robe
and took a call, and we knew
it was time to take you
half the globe home. And now,
when the Doubts arise, fears
for a world of bombs and spores
and mandatory veils, I nuzzle
my long nose along your tan chest
while chanting my own bass tune,
a maneuver that never fails
to elicit a startled laugh,
and your legs pedal the temperate air,
and your anklets chinkle,
and the thin red cord
the monk tied to your left wrist
gleams brighter than any gold,
telling us all goes well, and will,
for you are home.

First Egg

And quickly comes that day when first
    we taste blueberry, broccoli, lamb, the wind,
        our eyes dilating pools of delight at the new.

So you savor this inaugural bit of egg
    I transfer from the whorls of my finger
        to the rosette that is your Rosetta Stone.

May only the sweet & the succulent
    pass your lips, you who would swallow
        whatever gleams before you—& all does,

errant & fixed, as you crawl your rounds
    in thrall to that inner compass of wonder.
        Rug & fringe & under-rug. Watermelon seed,

dog food pellet, cat hair tumbleweeding
    the hard wood. May the world welcome you
        to its domains & dominions, as you welcome it.

May fear dally. May you forgive me
    my fecklessness, for I can do no more
        than to launch you like those little boats

of pale pink & powder blue I'd launch
    after a sudden summer storm: redolent
        of sidewalk dust & mown grass, rainwater,

pulsed from the faraway sky, gathers
   the wind-torn twigs & washes them
      toward the sewer, & with them sails

the paper boat, which knows the exhilaration
   of the wild ride, but not yet the destination.

Bad Buddhist

Our house is infested
     with these tiny moths, annoying
          as they are harmless.

Dancing madly in the evening
     light the way I imagine
          dance the Gypsies their kin

are named for, they converge
     upon me while I chop garlic,
          a plague of wings,

brown & black & bad
     Buddhist that I am, anger
          flares like a burst

of tracers in a night sky,
     so I do my best
          to kill all that I can.

A hard job, this eliminating
     your enemies
          one at a time & no matter

how many you whack, more
     appear. No wonder
          we invented Agent Orange,

not all that long after
     we dropped the Bomb.

Conundrum

Where did the whole world
come from, Daddy,
and all the countries and all the people
and the paper towels and lightbulbs?

One day the gurgle, the next the girl
with small fingers of joy
in the sounds of *hopscotch, bungee, budge*
securely interlaced with yours.

Why then this flutter within the thorax,
the gunmetal streaks
marring the aquamarine lagoon,
the cold scrutiny of the border guards?

Passing Customs

Returning home from Malawi
(place my daughter calls *meowie*),
I have nothing more to declare

than the 10 million who live there
declare of the spit-polished virus
goose-stepping through one in six

adults: they say little, complain less,
take solace in the lilting contrapuntal
mix of electrified African rock-and-roll

upon which the people's power
to exorcise the recurring specter
of the next week's goodbyes (sibling

parent lover spouse cousin neighbor friend)
alone depends, for though the stormtroopers
may be garrisoned, and the funerals proper,

so the bereaved can gather and grieve,
prayer can be called, chanted, read, still
the tracks to the crematoria go unbombed.

Picnic Near Camp Lejeune

The horseflies thicken our space
　　　at the seaside park, so she commands
　　　　　me to *Get the flyswapper*, this little one

who won't eat meat, as meat is flesh.
　　　And I swear the very moment I grasp
　　　　　the holey tool she'd have me wield,

eight military choppers buzz into ear-
　　　shot, rip the placid noonday sky apart,
　　　　　machine-gun needle-nose napalm-noise

death-tattoo spit-spray: adrenaline-rush
　　　even to this middle class–insulated, white-
　　　　　hued noncombatant. She screams out

not from fear but unalloyed delight,
　　　birthright of the well-tempered child,
　　　　　I know what they're doing, why they're there,

this startlingly muscled Cambodian
　　　girl screams out to her mother above
　　　　　the din—*they're having a helicopter race.*

Papaya

Your first three-syllable word
        and just to commit it to screen
                as I do here is utter violation

of today's aesthetic dictates—
        too cute, too endearing, *verboten*
                emotion given the scorched wings

and skulls that continue to accrue
        21 centuries post J-Christ's birth,
                but none of it will survive even

your second year, no matter
        how lovely the flutter and loop,
                Postman, Blue Morpho, Tiger

Longwing, airborne pacifiers all,
        elusive zephyrs dipsy-doodled
                about your tousled black hair,

thus I set it down, internal editor
        be damned: *butterfwhy, butterfwhy, butter-
        fwhy,* so when you read this some day,

long after our weekly jaunt to the Life
        & Science Museum has metamorphosed
                to barre, pointe, arabesque, plié, it'll be

preserved in this little chrysalis: sheen
        of glistening wings, shower of mist
                (artificially produced, yes, but mist

nonetheless) suffusing the air,
    temperature held to a steady 84,
        the myriad pests kept in check

by the darting, Crayola-green
    ground fowl you tirelessly pursue,
        the slices of papaya, giving succor

still.

FOUR

Heaven

Poetry //
Exceeding music must take the place
Of empty heaven and its hymns
　　　　—Wallace Stevens
　　　　"The Man with the Blue Guitar"

Oui, mon ami, a mean estate, devoid
of Chuckles (the lemon, the lime).

No zoot-suited organist sluicing fear
through Saturday Silents matinees,

no escaping that scrim of mute
smiling seraphim, no lush lutes

resounding across verdant buttes.
Nothing save prayer prayer prayer.

Yet when we attend with our inner-
most ear, we hear this plangent note:

the cry of the Earth's latest neonate—
that does suffice, that and the ineffable

joy we find in rhyming, say, *guitar*
with *catarrh,* or *squeegee* with *Ouija.*

The Unknown Albeit, or While Reading a Friend's Prizewinning
Book on Love's Vicissitudes He Writes About Words

—*for Robert Thomas*

Rhachis, dumka, grisette, iku, kulich, azagur—
    you're doing it again, amigo, sending me
        to meaning, avid as ever. So I enter *aa*

at www.Dictionary.com, find neither
    anti-aircraft nor Associate in Arts, but lava
        having a rough surface, though transmuted

in your hands to something *glorious, black-*
    faceted, trillion-spined. Rolling, I enter *trillion,*
        imagining hothouse blooms, forgetting

those twelve zeroes trailing the lonely one.
    Well, who wouldn't be confused by now,
        being confronted by the unknown albeit

mellifluous *mokihana,* lovely double spondee
    you've wed to *Mt. Waialeale,* a site looming
        above a leper colony in Tonga or Vanuatu

or Fiji, no doubt, but leading me to desire
    a dish of *wahine . . .* or is it *haole?* Never mind,
        here comes *szatmari,* your next seductress,

flashing skirts, black boots, scarlet lace,
    some ecstatic dance that sizzles and burns,
        I surmise, for your book's fiery and on *love,*

its tang and its char, the one subject I learned
    to shun like it's the electric prod, I'm the bum
        steer. But even the eReference is stumped,

though helpless it's not. Thus I'm queried
    do I intend *Satu Mare,* and lo!, a click away
        arises a medieval walled city in Transylvania,

setting for Stoker's gothic horror novel
    whose vampire lends his name to a bevy
        of diminutive tropical plants (genus *Dracula*)

having bizarre, sinister-looking purple flowers
    with pendulous scapes and hyper-motile lips—
        which sounds like the love I would write about

if I wrote about love, which is why I don't, but
    it's sure good to know when I reject *Satu Mare*
        there's still *stammerer* and *stud mare* left for me

to consider, and I do.

Phlox

And only in the light of lost words
Can we imagine our rewards
　　　　　—John Ashbery,
　　　　　"The Picture of Little J.A. in a Prospect of Flowers"

Such light in the words, does it matter
you're in the dark before the *res* itself?
It's like when the Odorama machines
faithfully reproduce the scent of sulfur
or subway or Chanel No. 5, but you never
took Chemistry, or bid Muskegon *adieu*—
which doesn't mean the vibrations triggered
by the chord pattern for freshly fallen snow
fail to evoke precisely the faintly falling flutter,
but that *loosestrife, larkspur, foxglove, asphodel*
tickle your cingulate gyrus or corpus callosum
or whatever plot of gray matter domiciles
those axonal sparkings of lexical delight
in the castanetting *ox-ox* of *gloxinia* and *phlox*
sans your having a clue if carmine or mauve
also inheres, let alone whether the spring
wind, chuffing across the ripening prairie,
rustles pistils that loose a sweet scent
over the oblivious herds of lowing cows.

Still

Still of the September night,
    still I limn your malachite eyes
        to the white noise of the window

unit smoothly cooling the attic. *Cool*
    you'd say when I'd say Sonny Rollins,
        tonight, the Blue Note, let's catch him

(cool always, whether playing clubs
    or jamming the Williamsburg Bridge).
        Today a friend confided his shortness

of breath whenever he climbs stairs
    and his wife's filing for divorce. Men,
        it's said, won't even hint at the intimate

to other men. Not true, they just need
    to be on the verge of suicide. You want
        a stress test, pal, and some counseling,

killing yourself's a nonviable option—
    there's your job, and your two little kids.
        She'll change her mind for sure, I lied.

When you're lying there alone
    in your attic bedroom, 4 A.M. and still
        you can't sleep, write an ode to her

eyes, to the cool latitude of her body
    atop yours. It'll be as close to truth
        as you'll ever get, you still want her

with every sweet smothered breath
      you can muster. It's the simple truth
          of the song from that distant country

station pumping its heat into the cool
      still air, pumping like a stalwart heart
          all the way from a Nashville studio

to a Brooklyn attic: you begin
      with *still,* move on to *cool,* follow
          it from there wherever it leads—

just don't forget the heart.

The Taste of Guava

What is that trace of a whine
that comes suddenly upon us
every once in a while from within
our inner ear, when we expect it least?
6 A.M., you're lying in your single bed,
logy yet somehow contemplative,
trying to recall the taste of guava
and whether *uhuru* is Swahili
for *freedom* or *no sweat*—and there
it is again, like a long-ago friend
making a cameo in your memory.
And though it doesn't rest on silent
haunches, it's about as close
as noise can come to silence,
and it departs as swiftly and silently
as any cat, leaving you more mystified
about everything, like why
Grandma always makes beef stew
on Veterans Day and why she persists
in garnishing her dishes with parsley
when it's so bitter—though it is,
come to think about it, quite a lovely
shade of deep, deep, green.

Dilemma

—*for Greg Rappleye*

A new acquaintance, Jim, just e-mailed me
    his reasons for no longer drinking coffee,
        having to do with dyspepsia, *Helicobacter,*

and imminence of his father's quadruple bypass,
    plus his need for a different job, his nonprofit
        also nonsupportive. Thus I find myself torn.

I could turn on the World Cup, or reply,
    commiserate, enquire has he too found Assam,
        Darjeeling, Earl Grey to be elixirs of renewal.

Ask if he thinks about the empire of *cha,*
    chai, thé, té, tea, and the way it's been built
        on the bent backs of the native planters

of Malaya, Sumatra, Borneo, Ceylon,
    their Indian overseers (and the distant owners),
        each living and life steeped in the dew-flecked

deep green leaves, their rolling and crushing.
    And isn't tea like garlic, can't be taken *too often*
        or *too strong*—the opposite dynamics at work

in the dismissal of U.S. Vice President
    Spiro T. Agnew, who, helicoptered into
        some Rust Belt spot in 1969 and offered

the chance to visit the local ghetto
    where the riots had occurred, demurred,
        "Seen one, done that." Social Darwinism

at its baddest. Which is all of a piece,
　　because last night Jim and I saw *Water,*
　　　　a film about a child bride (wed when 7)

who's just been widowed (age 8) and thus
　　has her long lustrous black hair sheared off
　　　　in an oxcart by her father and is condemned

never again to see her family, never to study
　　or marry or mother or wear her black hair long—
　　　　the widows' lot in India in 1938, the lucky ones

not cast onto the funeral pyre, the rite of suttee
　　not the karmic lot of upper-caste Brahmins
　　　　(who five millennia ago wrote the code),

albeit nothing could stop her grieving
　　illiterate father from delivering her up
　　　　to the distant cloister in the distant town.

Candor and rigor demand one call out cliché,
　　cull as one can, but I do have a brown daughter
　　　　soon to turn 7, as does Jim. So too the film ends

on hope for this spirited engaging girl
　　we've come to know and will not forget,
　　　　since the strong adult widow-protagonist

hands her to the handsome, well-educated
　　Gandhi disciple, who, having lost his beloved
　　　　fiancée to suicide (due to her sense of honor,

because for many years this beautiful widow
　　had supported the cloister by turning tricks,
　　　　and her chief patron, as Art demands of Fate,

had been the disciple's father), is leaning out
　　from the symbolic train to Delhi and the future,
　　　　where he will join Gandhi's passive resistance

against the Brits. (Meanwhile, in another part
    of the unspooling globe, Guernica and blitzkrieg
        and *der Führer* instruct the world in the necessary

calibration of evil, thus must hiatus be declared
    by the Mahatma [who, asked his views on *Western*
        Civilization, said *It would be a good idea*], the unyoking

of India from the English Raj not occur until 1947,
    Pakistan, "Land of the Pure," breeched en passant
        into being, communal exchange fueled by differing

affiliations killing lakhs, crores.) Gandhi will reiterate
    that the plight of Indian widows must be redressed,
        one reason he's assassinated by "Hindu fanatics,"

all this transpiring in a cinematic tomorrow
    as well as the irrecoverable past. The epilogue
        of *Water* tells us today, at the onset of a new

millennium, 35 million widows still live
    this way, which explains the film's being
        an object of violence by devout hands

enraged by besmirchment of their Gods
    (all incarnations of one god). So it destines,
        so it coheres, given place, given persons

(and their respective organs of generation),
    given the cause, given effect, in the men
        and in the religion that reigns in the men,

and vice versa, men that might hug
    their daughters yet shear their hair
        when their good book commands,

that might detonate the car bomb
    or yank the pin from the hand grenade.

Air and All

It's no gift,
this seeing through
to the emptiness
all things possess.
The tallest oak:
nothing
but empty space. Mor
of forest floor,
liana thick
as a man's waist,
the oceans vast:
empty space.

Sure,
there's the entire
benthic realm—
phytoplankton
& a few sperm whales
cruising the fracture
zone—but mostly
there's the pair
of O's & the H, the N:
space between,
space within.

What, too,
are the noctilucent
clouds,
or your iliac crest,
your malar eminence.
What

fills the distance
between us
& faint Boötes
(the Herdsman:
white motes
in the farthest
northern sky).

Yes, empty
space
is the vacant
lot of God—
but *damn,*
these roasted
red peppers
taste fine,
mighty fine,
water & air
& all.

If They Don't Have Ritalin in Heaven,

I guess I'll be up there with all of them,
 Allah, Krishna, Yahweh, God, speeding
  along, shooting the shit with the Hims,

asking Him and Him do they too love
 the names of these rivers the way I do,
  Irrawaddy, Orinoco, Limpopo, Snake,

the banyans & cottonwoods & teaks
 that overhang their banks, salmon & pike
  that teem beneath—& isn't it great how

piano in Papuan Pidgin is *big black box*
 with teeth you hit him he cry, & even though
  the mosquito transmits malaria & dengue

& thus has vexed untold millions unto
 this day, & the spirochete causes yaws,
  aren't both elegant beings—the angel-

winged tuning-fork vibrato of the former;
 the latter so sinuous & svelte & beguiling
  under the scope—& speaking of speeding,

what about that Audi Quattro, how it accelerates,
 0 to 60 in 5.3 seconds (though you're definitely
  playing dice with your life when you tool out

onto the Beltway into the morning rush,
 flitting between those minivans & cement
  mixers, 18-wheelers & SUVs), & if you stop

to think about it, what's the hurry anyway—
    the *Times* reports 97% of American workers
        say they'd quit their jobs in a trice if they hit

the lottery. (Me, I always play numbers
    3, 17, & 1789, in honor of Saint Patrick
        & of Voltaire, Rousseau, & the other lights

of the French Revolution, those *philosophes*
    sans whose Rights of Man we'd be spinning
        purposelessly atop the fragile tectonic plates

atop the hissing molten core.) I guess it'll take
    a week or two for me to get back to the Hims
        (nary a molecule of Ritalin lacing the cocktail

that is my blood), but when I finally arrive
    maybe I won't shoot the shit after all, not
        babble about the baobabs, the Monongahela,

maybe I'll just sit still there & regard
    the dread shape, the fearsome visage
        (cross between an Ayatollah & a Mather,

I imagine, proving the imagination
    is influenced unduly by the news media
        & by high school), & for the good of all

I'll stare into His remorseless eye & enquire
    if indeed the Existentialists had gotten it right,
        He'd created this world, then given it up, cast

His lot elsewhere, out there past
    the moons of Pluto, sick as He was
        of our whining & scribbling & warring—

though admit it, didn't He sometimes miss
    the water hyacinth floating swiftly along
        the Mekong after the rains, the ineffable

downward curve of the weeping willows,
    the intoxicating scent of jasmine at dusk,
        Mozart's Clarinet Concerto in A Major,

& the dinosaurs.

About the Author

Roy Jacobstein is the acclaimed author of the poetry collections *A Form of Optimism, Tourniquet, Ripe,* and *Blue Numbers, Red Life.* He has received the James Wright Prize, the Felix Pollak Prize, and the Morse Poetry Prize. His poetry has appeared in many publications, including the *Threepenny Review,* the *Southern Review, TriQuarterly,* and the *Journal of the American Medical Association.* Jacobstein is a public health physician who lives with his wife and daughter in Chapel Hill, North Carolina.